Design and Make
PICTURE
FRAMES

Susie Hodge

A+

Smart Apple Media

Contents

Framing pictures.........................4

Be prepared............................6

Jeweled frame.........................8

Printed frame.......................10

Family tree............................12

Art Deco frame....................14

A handy clothespin 16

Fishy fabric frame..............18

 Golden pasta frame..............20

Embroidered frame..............22

 Far-out foam!..................24

Sculptured fruit frame.......26

Mosaic frame................28

Glossary and
further information......30

Index......32

Framing pictures

This book shows you how to create your own unique picture frames using things you can find around your home. You can make a golden frame, like one for a famous painting in a gallery, or even design a frame to display your whole family tree!

Why do we frame pictures?

Why do you think we put pictures in frames? Think about what picture frames in your home look like. How do you think they make pictures or photos look different? Do they make the picture stand out more? Or is the frame a feature in itself?

The way a picture is framed and the design and material used can be as important as the picture itself. In the 15th century, artists

painted on wooden panels and built up the frames directly on the wood using a mixture of glue and chalk.

As artists began to paint on canvas instead of panels, the frame became a separate object attached to the finished painting. Frames became an expensive feature, designed not only to enhance the painting, but also to show off the skills of the woodcarver and gilder.

New ideas

In the late 19th and early 20th centuries, artists began to use frames that related more to their paintings. Artists such as Vincent van Gogh and Georges Seurat often decorated their frames to match the painting. Some artists removed the frame altogether, believing that frames separated the painting from the viewer. More recent artists have explored the idea of making the frame part of the picture.

Le Chahut by Georges Seurat

Photographs

The invention of photography in 1839 meant a new type of picture was displayed. Victorian society loved the idea that people could have a family portrait without it costing them a fortune. Today, we have frames for all types of pictures. They can be elegant, cute, or funny. Whether you are making frames for yourself or as a present, think about personalizing them and making them suit the picture.

Mounting and protecting

The simplest way to frame a picture is to attach, or mount, it onto colored paper or tagboard. When you mount a picture, choose a color that blends well with the picture and makes it look good. Framed pictures are often mounted as well. Sometimes they are protected by glass or plastic, too. Think about whether or not you are going to mount the pictures you put in your frames and how you are going to protect them.

Be prepared

These two pages show you all the different materials and equipment you will need to make the frames in this book.

When you're making a frame:

✻ Keep everything you need in a large box or in a corner of your room.

✻ Collect the materals gradually; there is no need to get everything at once.

✻ Never let paint or glue dry on your brushes—always wash them carefully in warm, soapy water and rinse and dry them well.

Things you need

Art foom

Self-hardening clay

A selection of tagboard, cardboard, and paper in different sizes, colors, and thicknesses

A selection of odds and ends, such as sequins, beads, newspapers, ribbon, clothespins, buttons, silver foil, small ceramic tiles, natural sponge, and pasta shapes

Scraps of cloth, including felt, embroidery fabric, and medium-weight fabrics that don't fray easily, cotton and embroidery thread

Shelf paper, acetate

Equipment

A compass and a T-square

Paints, especially poster or acrylic paints and any metallic colors

Double-sided tape, clear tape, and masking tape

Felt-tip pens and colored pencils

Paint brushes

Craft glue

Craft knife, cutting board, and strong ruler

You will need some paper towels for cleaning up and an apron or old shirt to protect your clothing

Scissors, assorted needles

Cutting cardboard

The best way to cut smooth, straight lines for frames is to use a craft knife. If you are going to cut in this way, you must use a cutting board and a strong ruler. Most importantly, you must ask an adult to help you—never cut in this way without adult supervision.

Start by placing your ruler on the line that you want to cut. Hold it there firmly, making sure that your fingers are well away from the edge of the ruler and from the knife. Cut by dragging the craft knife along the edge of the ruler, using the ruler to steady the knife and making sure that your fingers are away from the blade at all times.

Jeweled frame

Using sequins, beads, glitter, and fake gems, make a frame fit for a king or queen.

Look at this!

The Byzantines created magnificent panels of gold encrusted with priceless jewels. This one is from the Pala D'Oro altarpiece in St Mark's in Venice, Italy.

✳ Why do you think they liked to use jewels and gold in their art?

Design and select

Design a glittering frame covered with jewels inspired by Byzantine art! Think about what you will use to make the frame and how you will decorate it. Draw a picture of your idea and select your materials—we've used cardboard, fake gems, beads, sequins, glitter, and gold paint.

Make

1 Choose the picture you want to frame. Use this as a guide to mark the size and shape of your frame and its "window" on a piece of cardboard. Cut out a piece of cardboard the same size as the frame to make the back. Set it aside.

2 Cut out your frame and paint it with metallic gold paint. Leave it to dry for a few hours.

3 Arrange your gems, jewels, and sequins on the frame and glue them in place when you are satisfied with your design. You could make a pattern or simply spread a thin layer of glue over the frame and sprinkle the gems on. Leave to dry so the jewels are held firmly in place.

Challenge
Make a "picture" around the frame, like a collage of sequins and glitter.

4 Measure and cut out three strips of cardboard to make "spacers." Glue these on the back of the frame (the cardboard you set aside earlier) as shown at right. Spacers hold your picture in place and let you slide it in and out of the frame. Carefully glue the front of the frame onto the spacers. Don't glue down the fourth side—this is where your picture slides in.

5 To make a stand for the frame, cut out a small rectangle of tagboard. Fold it into three and unfold again. Glue the top third of the tagboard onto the back of the frame, about halfway up. When the glue is dry, insert your picture, stand the frame up, and dazzle everyone!

9

Printed frame

Make a double frame inspired by nature to please someone special!

Look at this!

Wrapping paper and wallpaper are often printed with natural forms, such as leaves and flowers.

✱ How do you think the leaf shapes were made?

✱ How can you make the pattern repeat?

Design and select

Design a simple double frame shape, scaling its length and width according to the size of picture you want to frame. Collect some leaves in different shapes and sizes, asking an adult for permission if you need to pick any of them. Think about the colors you will use to decorate the frame. Select your materials—we've used thick tagboard for the frame, cardboard for the back of the frame, leaves, and paint.

Make

1 Cut out a long rectangle of thick cardboard for the back of your frame, based on your design. With a craft knife, lightly score a vertical line down the middle on the back. Be careful not to cut all the way through. This will allow you to fold the frame like a book so that it will stand up.

2 Cut four thin strips of cardboard about half an inch (1.3 cm) wide to go down the sides of the frame, and two thicker strips to go along the bottom as spacers. Glue to the back of the frame as shown.

3 To make the front frames, cut out two pieces of thick tagboard to fit on each side of the cardboard back.

4 Cover your work surface with newspaper. Paint the frame fronts a pale color. Using darker colors, paint the underside of some of the leaves you collected. Gently press down the painted side of the leaves onto your frames to create a printed pattern.

Challenge
What else could you use for printing? How about natural sponges, lace, or textured material? How could you create a stenciled design instead?

5 When the paint is dry, cut out two pieces of transparent acetate and tape them to the back of your printed frames over the windows. This will protect your pictures. Glue the printed frames onto the folding back along the spacer bars and insert your pictures.

Family tree

Display pictures of your whole family in one frame.

Design and select

Design a picture frame that can show your entire family at once—as many people and pets as you choose! We based our design on a family tree. Draw a picture of your idea. Think about the materials you could use—we've used cardboard, paints, and acetate.

Make

1. Copy the outline of your design onto a strong piece of cardboard to make the front of the frame and cut out carefully. Cut out a piece of cardboard exactly the same shape for the back of the frame and set it aside.

Challenge
What other designs could you use to display your whole family?

2. Use a compass to draw enough circles on the frame front for your family members. Make sure they are big enough for the photos. Ask an adult to help you cut out the circles using a craft knife or scissors. Now, place the frame front on the frame back and draw around the inside of the circles so you know where to place the photos.

3 Cut out your photos, place them in the right position on the frame back, and secure them using double-sided tape. You can make a photocopy of a photograph if you don't want to cut up the original.

Challenge
What other ways could you hold the pictures in place? Could you design a frame where the pictures slide in and out?

4 Paint the front of the frame using browns and greens and allow it to dry.

Challenge
How could you make the tree three-dimensional?

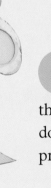

5 Attach a sheet of acetate to the back of the frame front using double-sided tape. This will protect your photographs.

6 Attach the front of the frame to the back using glue or tape. Make a stand for your family tree out of a triangular piece of cardboard with an extra flap on one edge to glue down. Now your family tree is ready to display.

Art Deco frame

Make an artistic frame out of stiff tagboard and shelf paper, using a famous design style as your inspiration.

Design and select

Design a frame out of shiny materials and contrasting colors. How many picture "windows" will it have? Will the frame stand up or hang from a wall? Design your frame on paper and select your materials— we've used stiff tagboard and metallic shelf paper.

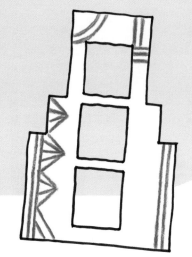

Make

1 Copy your design onto a large piece of tagboard and cut it out. Make an exact copy of the frame shape for the back and set it aside.

2 On the frame front, draw your "windows." You could make these different shapes and sizes depending on the pictures you want to display. Ask an adult to help you cut out the windows with a craft knife.

3 To decorate your frame, cut out some shelf paper that is about an inch (2.5 cm) wider than the frame all the way around. Fold the shelf paper around your tagboard frame and tape or glue it down neatly. Carefully smooth out any air bubbles.

✱ Tip: you will find it easier to cover corners if you cut small triangles from each corner of the shelf paper. Cut a cross inside each window and fold back the shelf paper.

Challenge
What material could you use instead of shelf paper?

4 Add detail to the frame by using shapes cut out of shelf paper in a contrasting color. Carefully stick these shapes onto your covered frame. Cut a strip of acetate and attach this behind the windows to protect your pictures.

5 Make spacers to fit between the front and back of the frame. Glue these strips on the edges of the back. Place your pictures in position.

6 Glue the frame front to the back. Make a stand for your frame out of a triangle of cardboard with an extra flap to glue down.

Challenge
Investigate a design style called Art Nouveau. Design a frame based on this.

A handy clothespin

A clothespin stand can be a handy way to display a piece of artwork or a photograph! It's so easy that we've made two picture holders.

Design and select

Design a picture holder based around a simple clothespin. Think about how you'll make the clothespin stand up and how you can decorate it. We've attached our clothespin to a "helping hand." Draw a sketch of your idea. Select your materials—we used colored tagboard, cardboard, and wooden clothespins.

Make

Challenge
How could you adapt a simple idea like this to make a refrigerator magnet?

1 On a sheet of colored tagboard, trace around each of your hands. Carefully cut out the two hand shapes.

Challenge
How could you adapt this frame to have mittens or gloves? How would you decorate them?

2 Using craft glue, attach a clothespin to the back of each hand so that the clip is at the top. This will hold your picture.

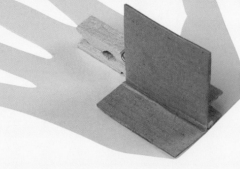

3 Make a stand for your frame from a rectangle of cardboard. Score a line down one side of it. Fold along the line and glue the narrower side next to the clothespin. Now, simply stand up the hand and clip in your photo!

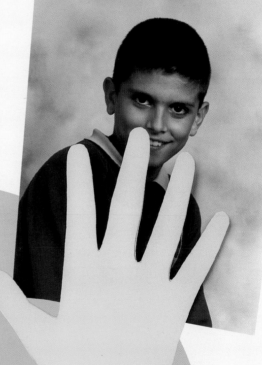

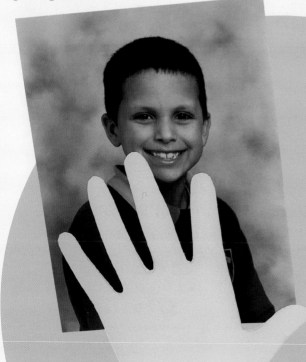

Challenge
Could you build up the surface of your hands, perhaps with crumpled paper, to make them three-dimensional?

Fishy fabric frame

A fabric frame with colorful fish on it makes a stunning border for a photograph or picture.

Design and select

Design a frame made of fabric, with appliqué pieces sewn or glued onto it. Think about what type of fabric you'll use and what your design will look like. Draw a picture of your idea and select your materials. We've used cardboard, felt, thread, ribbons, sequins, and glitter.

Make

1 Based on your drawing, cut out some shapes for your design in your chosen fabric. We've made a sea-themed frame.

Challenge
What other scene could you design for this frame? What about a wild jungle?

2 Draw your frame on some cardboard and cut it out. Cut out a piece of fabric that is big enough to cover both sides of your frame. Sew it together neatly at the edges and corners.

Challenge
How could you pad the frame or make 3D fish?

18

3 Sew or glue your sea creatures onto the covered frame. Add some thin, shiny ribbons curling upward to look like seaweed. Use sequins and glitter for the fish eyes and air bubbles.

Challenge
How else could you make your picture look like it's underwater?

4 Attach a piece of acetate to the back of the frame front. This will add to the underwater effect. Cut out a piece of cardboard the same size as the front to make the back. Glue the front and back together leaving the top side unglued so you can insert a picture (the fabric acts like spacers).

5 Cut out a small rectangle of tagboard to make the stand. Fold the top third and glue this part onto the back of the frame, in the middle. Put a picture inside your finished fabric frame that matches the theme!

Golden pasta frame

This frame resembles the heavy golden frames that you often see on antique paintings. Using simple objects, you can make expensive-looking frames for all your pictures.

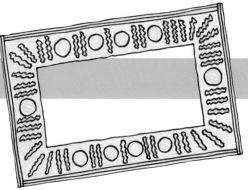

Design and select

Design a golden frame that looks expensive and striking. What sort of picture suits this frame, and what could you use to decorate it? Draw a picture of your idea. Select your materials—we used cardboard, pasta shapes, and gold paint.

Make

1   Using a ruler, mark out your frame on a piece of cardboard and cut it out carefully. Don't forget to cut out the window, too. Cut out another piece of cardboard the same size for the back of the frame.

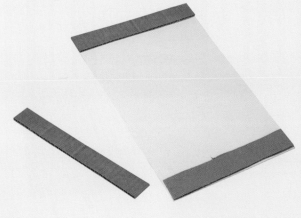

2   Cut out three cardboard spacers for your frame. Carefully glue or tape these on the bottom and sides of the back of the frame. Make sure your spacers do not stick out farther than the edge of the frame.

3 Select your pasta shapes—use different sizes and shapes to give your frame lots of texture. Arrange them in a pattern on the cardboard frame and secure them using craft glue. Allow to dry.

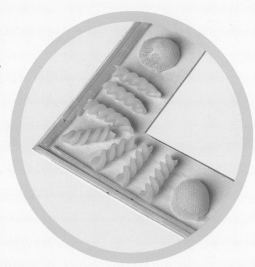

Challenge
What could you use other than pasta to create texture on the frame?

4 Using gold paint and a medium thickness paint brush, paint the frame, the pasta shapes, and any other embellishments you've included. Be sure to cover all the edges and difficult areas. Give the frame a couple of coats of paint, allowing it to dry between each one.

Challenge
How could you make your frame a more unusual shape, like the one on page 20?

5 When the gold paint is dry, glue the front to the back of the frame and insert a picture. Make a simple hook so that the frame can be hung on a wall (see page 25).

Challenge
How could you make this frame stand up instead of hang on a wall?

Embroidered frame

Make a padded, embroidered frame. You could use all sorts of stitches and colored embroidery thread or even shiny gold thread. Try personalizing it by adding a name!

Design and select

Design an embroidered frame for your room. Think about what you will embroider and what colors and materials you will use. Sketch out your idea and select your materials. We used tagboard, batting, embroidery fabric, and gold embroidery thread.

Make

1 Draw the size and shape of your frame on a piece of stiff tagboard, making sure it is big enough to fit your chosen picture. Ask an adult to help you cut this out carefully with scissors or a craft knife.

2 Place the frame shape onto a piece of fabric to figure out how much material you need. Draw lightly around the inside and outside of the frame with a pencil to mark the area you will embroider. Draw another line around the outside edge of the frame adding an extra inch (2.5 cm).

3 To cut out the window in the fabric, cut diagonally across from corner to corner to make four flaps. Then, cut out the frame following the outside pencil line. Now you can begin to embroider.

4 Choose your embroidery thread and tie a knot in one end. Thread the other end through a large needle. Following your pencil marks so you know where to embroider, sew through one hole in the fabric and across and through a hole diagonally opposite. From the back, sew diagonally through the opposite side to make a little "X." Repeat the pattern all over the embroidery area.

5 Cut out some batting, the exact size and shape of the frame, and glue it to the frame. Now, glue your embroidered fabric around the frame, folding in the flaps of material and making sure you match up the edges.

Challenge
Make a frame using ribbons sewn on the fabric instead of embroidery. How will you use the ribbons?

6 Make the back of the frame with spacers as on page 9. Attach the front of the frame to the back and make a stand (if you want the frame to stand up rather than hang). Insert your picture.

Far-out foam!

Make a frame out of colored foam shapes. Foam can be bought in all colors in craft shops and is easy to work with. It can make your frames look very professional!

Design and select

Design a frame based on outer space. Think about what shapes you will cut out to decorate the frame, and draw a picture of your idea. Select your materials— we used tagboard and colored foam.

Make

1 Draw the size and shape of your frame on a piece of colored foam. You might want to think about what color will suit your idea best. Draw the shape of your "window" on the foam and cut it out.

Challenge
What other shapes could you use for the "window" of your frame?

2 Think about the shapes you will use to decorate your frame. You might need to sketch them first. Copy your sketches onto some foam and carefully cut out the shapes.

Challenge
Make different shapes out of the foam instead—what about letters or numbers for a different theme?

3 Place your space shapes on your foam frame. Try different arrangements before you glue them on. When you are satisfied with your design, attach them with craft glue.

4 Cut out a slightly larger foam frame in a contrasting color. Cut a window in it and glue it to the back of your decorated frame.

5 Make the back of the frame (see pages 8 and 9). Add a hook to the back using a folded piece of tagboard with a hole cut in it. Glue the frame together, insert your picture, and hang it up!

Sculptured fruit frame

A frame becomes a work of art when you sculpt tiny, handmade fruits to decorate it. Look at pictures of famous still-life paintings to get some ideas.

Design and select

Design a picture frame that is as creative and artistic as any picture that will go inside it. Consider what you will use to build up the sculpture, or relief, and draw a picture of your idea. Think about what materials you might use—we've used self-hardening clay, paints, and cardboard.

Make

1 Base your frame on the drawing you made. Cut out the shape of your frame from stiff cardboard. We drew around a plate to make the frame, but you could use a compass to make your circles instead.

2 Draw a smaller circle in the center of your frame. Ask an adult to help you cut it out carefully using scissors or a craft knife and cutting board.

3 Using the clay, or whatever material you have chosen to make the decorations, sculpt the tiny fruit shapes. When these are dry, paint them carefully in fruit colors.

Challenge
What could you use instead of clay to make the sculpted shapes for your frame?

26

4 Paint your frame. When it is dry, add the painted fruits to your frame with craft glue.

Challenge
What other fruits or objects could you make?

5 Cut a sheet of acetate into a circle and attach it to the back of the frame using craft glue or double-sided tape.

6 Cut out a matching cardboard circle for the back of the frame. Create a spacer as shown using another semi-circle of cardboard. Glue the frame together and add a hook or hinge. Now put your fabulously framed picture on display!

Challenge
Make a similar frame, but decorate with candy.

Mosaic frame

Mosaics are very easy to make and very artistic. People have made mosaics for centuries, but they are still fashionable!

Design and select

Design a picture frame using ceramic tiles. Think about the kind of mosaic you will make. Will it be a set pattern, a picture, or in a particular color scheme? Draw a picture of your idea, then think about what materials you might use—we've used small square ceramic tiles, cardboard, and plaster.

Make

1 Draw the shape of your frame on a piece of firm cardboard. Use a ruler for the sides if necessary, and measure the frame to make sure that your tiles will fit side by side, or however you choose to arrange them.

2 Ask an adult to help you cut out your frame carefully using sharp scissors or a craft knife and cutting board. Spread glue on the frame in small sections and begin to apply your tiles carefully, moving around the frame, covering one section at a time. Let the glue dry.

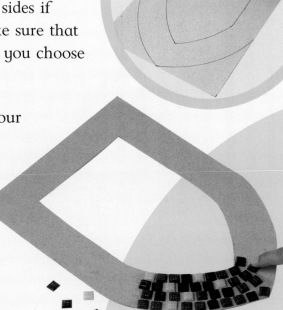

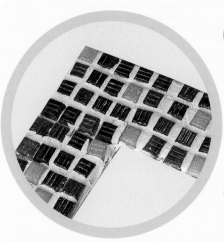

3 When the glue has dried, you might want to plaster between the tiles to fill in any gaps. Plaster is soft, white powder that, when mixed with water, forms a kind of cement. Spread the wet plaster over the tiles and push it down between them. Wipe the excess mixture off the tiles and allow to dry.

4 Cut out the frame shape from a sheet of acetate and glue it to the underside of the frame.

5 To make the back of the frame, cut out two pieces of cardboard the same shape as the front and glue together. The double thickness of cardboard will support the heavy tiles better. Attach two spacers to the sides of the frame and one to the bottom.

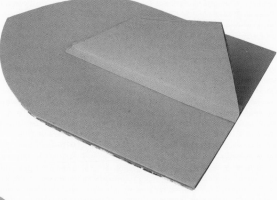

6 To make the frame stand up, cut out two cardboard shapes with a diagonal edge (shown above) and glue them together. Leave a flap on either side to fold back and glue onto the frame back. Assemble all the parts and put a picture inside your mosaic frame!

Challenge
What else could you use instead of ceramic tiles? How about things you would usually recycle?

29

Glossary

acetate
a clear sheet of flexible material (called cellulose acetate)

appliqué
fabric pieces applied to other material

batting
soft stuffing

Byzantine
from the Eastern Roman Empire, A.D. 395 to 1453; Its capital was Byzantium (later Constantinople and now Istanbul in Turkey)

canvas
a rough cloth made from hemp or cotton that can be painted on when stretched tightly

complement
things that go together, such as colors

embroidery
decorative needlework

embroidery fabric
fabric with holes already in it for embroidery

geometric
designs made up of simple shapes and lines

gilder
a craftsman who specializes in covering surfaces, such as wood or plaster, in gold or gold-colored paint or material

hinge
a joint that bends

metallic
shiny, resembling metal

plaster
a white powder that, when mixed with water, forms a kind of cement; Plaster is used to fill in cracks in walls or gaps between tiles

relief
a picture or design that is raised up from a flat surface

repeat pattern
a pattern that is repeated across a design

spacers
strips of cardboard that are attached between the front and back of a frame on three sides only, leaving one side open to insert a picture

stencil
a sheet of tagboard with shapes cut out of it used to make a pattern

three-dimensional
having three dimensions: length, width, and depth

transparent
see-through

Further information

There are many different types of frames on display in galleries and museums, featuring both paintings and photographs. Notice how the frames complement the images within them. They have either been specially made or specifically selected for each picture.

Here is a selection of galleries and museums to visit:

The Metropolitan Museum of Art
New York, New York
www.metmuseum.org

Art Institute of Chicago
Chicago, Illinois
www.artic.edu

Smithsonian
Washington, D.C.
www.si.edu

Museum of Fine Arts, Boston
Boston, Massachusetts
www.mfa.org

National Gallery of Art
Washington, D.C.
www.nga.gov

Los Angeles County Museum of Art
Los Angeles, California
www.lacma.org

National Gallery of Canada
Ontario, Canada
www.national.gallery.ca

The Getty Center
Los Angeles, California
www.getty.edu

Index

acetate 11, 12, 13, 15, 19, 27, 29
appliqué 18

batting 23
beads 6, 8
Byzantine 8, 29

cardboard 6, 8, 10, 11, 12, 13, 16, 17, 18, 19, 20, 21, 25, 26, 28
clay 6, 26, 27
clothespin 16, 17
compass 7, 12, 26
craft glue 7, 9, 17, 25, 27, 28
craft knife 7, 10, 12, 14, 22, 26, 28

fabric 6, 18, 22, 23
family portrait 5
  tree 4, 12, 13
felt 6, 18
flowers 10
foam 6, 24, 25
frames
  Art Deco 14, 15
  embroidered 22, 23
  far-out foam 24, 25
  fishy fabric 18, 19
  golden pasta 20, 21
  handy clothespin 16, 17
  jeweled 8, 9
  mosaic 28, 29
  printed 10, 11
  reasons for 4
  sculptured fruit 26, 27

gallery 4
Gaudi, Antoni 28
gems 8, 9
gilder 4, 29
glass 5, 28
glitter 8, 9, 18, 19
gold
  frames 4, 20, 21
  paint 8, 20, 21

Greece 8

hinge 9, 27
hook 21, 25, 27

jewels 9

leaves 10, 11

mount 5

paint 7, 10, 11, 12, 13, 26, 27
paper 5, 6
photograph 4, 5, 12, 13, 16, 17, 18
plaster 28, 29
plastic 5

ribbon 6, 18, 19, 23

scissors 7, 22, 26, 28

sequins 6, 8, 9, 18, 19
Seurat, Georges 5
shelf paper 6, 14, 15
spacers 8, 11, 15, 20, 23, 25, 27, 29
stand 13, 15, 17, 19

tagboard 5, 6, 10, 11, 12, 14, 16, 19, 20, 22, 24, 28, 29
tape 7
  double-sided 13, 27
thread 18
  embroidery 22, 23
  gold 22
Tutankhamun 14

van Gogh, Vincent 5

window 8, 14, 15, 20, 24, 25
woodcarver 4

First published in 2005 by
Franklin Watts, 96 Leonard Street
London EC2A 4XD

Franklin Watts Australia
Level 17/207 Kent Street, Sydney, NSW 2000

This edition published under license from Franklin Watts. All rights reserved.

Copyright © 2005 Franklin Watts

Editor: Rachel Tonkin; **Art Director:** Jonathan Hair;
Design: Matthew Lilly; **Photography:** Steve Shott.
Picture credits: Albright-Knox Art Gallery/Corbis: 5t. Basilica San Marco Venice /Dagli Orti/
Art Archive: 8t. Robert Harding Picture Library/Alamy: 14t. Image Farm Inc/Alamy: 20t.
Andrew Morse/Alamy: 28t. V & A Images/Alamy: 4c, 4b.
With thanks to Jack and Thomas Lilly D'Cruz and Peter Holmes for the use of their drawings.

Published in the United States by Smart Apple Media
2140 Howard Drive West, North Mankato, Minnesota 56003

U.S. publication copyright © 2007 Smart Apple Media
International copyright reserved in all countries. No part of this book may be reproduced in any form
without written permission from the publisher.
Printed in the United States of America

Library of Congress Cataloging-in-Publication Data

Hodge, Susie, 1960-
Picture frames / by Susie Hodge.
p. cm. — (Design and make)
Includes index.
ISBN-13 : 978-1-58340-953-4
1. Picture frames and framing—Juvenile literature. 2. Decoration and ornament—
Juvenile literature. I. Title. II. Design and make (North Mankato, Minn.)

TT899.2.H64 2006
749'.7—dc22   2005052051

2 4 6 8 9 7 5 3 1